SWEET

Bounty Books and ACP Magazines Ltd hereby
exclude all liability to the extent permitted by law for
any errors or omissions in this book and for any loss,
damage or expense (whether direct or indirect) suffered
by a third party relying on any information contained
in this book.

First published in 2007 by ACP Magazines Ltd

This edition published in 2011 by Bounty Books,
a division of Octopus Publishing Group Ltd,
Endeavour House, 189 Shaftesbury Avenue, London WC2H 8JY
www.octopusbooks.co.uk

An Hachette UK Company
www.hachette.co.uk

Copyright © ACP Magazines Ltd 2007

ISBN: 978-0-753722-29-9

Printed and bound in China

THE AUSTRALIAN
Women's Weekly

SWEET

Bounty
BOOKS

contents

In just one
delicious mouthful, the
delicacies in this heavenly book
will whisk you away to sugary paradise.
Divine sweets, the most perfect, wobbling
vanilla slice, exquisite little bombes of fluffy
sugar, soft, warm fudges and delicate choux
pastry – all to be eaten in one breathtaking
bite. These wonderful little treasures are chic
accompaniments to serve with coffee or tea,
or they're just as delicious when stolen
straight from the baking tray – either
way, these miniature morsels are
a sweet sensation.

chocolate fudge

It is important to use a sugar thermometer in this recipe (see pg 120) to get the correct consistency when making the fudge.

1½ cups (330g) caster sugar
½ cup (110g) firmly packed
   brown sugar
60g dark eating chocolate,
   chopped coarsely
2 tablespoons glucose syrup
½ cup (125ml) double cream
¼ cup (60ml) milk
40g unsalted butter, chopped

1 Grease deep 15cm-square cake tin; line base with baking parchment, extending paper 5cm over sides.
2 Combine sugars, chocolate, syrup, cream and milk in small heavy-based saucepan; stir over heat, without boiling, until sugar dissolves. Bring to a boil; boil, uncovered, without stirring, about 10 minutes or until syrup reaches 116°C on sugar thermometer.
3 Remove pan from heat immediately, leave sugar thermometer in the syrup; add butter, do not stir.
4 Cool fudge about 20 minutes or until the temperature of the syrup drops to 40°C; remove sugar thermometer.
5 Stir fudge with wooden spoon about 10 minutes or until a small amount dropped from the spoon will hold its shape.
6 Quickly spread fudge into tin; cover with foil. Stand at room temperature about 3 hours or until fudge sets.
7 Lift fudge out of tin; cut into squares.

makes 49

minted chocolate creams

You need 25 foil petit four cases for this recipe.

100g white eating chocolate, melted
2 tablespoons whipping cream
200g dark eating chocolate, melted
peppermint oil or essence
green food colouring
¼ cup (35g) roasted unsalted pistachios, chopped finely

1 Combine white chocolate and cream in small bowl; refrigerate filling about 1 hour or until thickened, stirring occasionally.
2 Meanwhile, using small clean, dry artists' brush, brush dark chocolate inside 25 petit four cases (see pg 117); place on tray, refrigerate until set.
3 Flavour filling with oil or essence to taste; tint with colouring.
4 Spoon filling into piping bag fitted with 5mm-fluted tube; pipe into chocolate cases. Carefully peel foil cases away from chocolate (see pg 117); sprinkle filling with nuts.

makes 25

turkish delight

It is important to use a sugar thermometer in this recipe (see pg 120) in order to get the correct consistency required for turkish delight.

¼ cup (45g) gelatine
¼ cup (60ml) water
3 cups (660g) caster sugar
2 cups (500ml) water, extra
¾ cup (110g) wheaten cornflour
2 tablespoons glucose syrup
50ml rosewater essence
red food colouring
⅔ cup (110g) icing sugar, sifted

1 Grease deep 19cm-square cake tin.
2 Sprinkle gelatine over the water in small jug; stand jug in small saucepan of simmering water. Stir until gelatine dissolves.
3 Combine caster sugar and ¾ cup of the extra water in medium saucepan; stir over heat, without boiling, until sugar dissolves. Bring to a boil; boil, without stirring, until temperature of the syrup reaches 116°C (soft ball) on sugar thermometer. Simmer at 116°C for 5 minutes, without stirring, regulating heat to maintain temperature at 116°C. Remove pan from heat.
4 Meanwhile, place cornflour in another medium saucepan; gradually blend in the remaining extra water. Bring to a boil, stirring, until mixture boils and thickens.

5 Gradually stir hot sugar syrup, gelatine mixture and glucose into cornflour mixture; bring to a boil, stirring. Reduce heat; simmer, stirring, about 10 minutes or until mixture thickens a little more. Remove pan from heat; whisk in rosewater, tint with colouring.
6 Strain mixture through fine sieve into cake tin; skim any scum from surface. Stand 15 minutes; cover surface with lightly greased baking parchment, stand overnight.
7 Turn turkish delight onto board dusted with icing sugar, dust with more icing sugar; cut with icing-sugar-coated-knife. Roll pieces in remaining icing sugar. Store turkish delight in an airtight container at room temperature for up to two weeks.

makes 48

You need 20 foil petit four cases for this recipe.

1 egg white
¼ cup (55g) caster sugar
2 teaspoons caster sugar, extra
1 tablespoon raspberry jam, warmed, sieved
2 teaspoons orange-flavoured liqueur
75g small strawberries, quartered

1 Preheat oven to 120°C/100°C fan-assisted. Place petit four cases on oven tray.
2 Beat egg white and 2 tablespoons of the sugar in small bowl with electric mixer until sugar is dissolved; fold in remaining 1 tablespoon sugar.
3 Drop rounded teaspoons of mixture into cases. Sprinkle meringues with extra sugar.
4 Bake about 25 minutes or until meringues are dry to touch. Cool meringues in oven with door ajar.
5 Meanwhile, combine jam and liqueur in small saucepan; stir over low heat until warm.
6 Gently press berries into top of each meringue; brush with warm jam mixture. Serve immediately.

makes 20

strawberry meringues

choc-mint slice

1 cup (220g) caster sugar
⅔ cup (160ml) evaporated milk
2 teaspoons glucose syrup
15g butter
100g white marshmallows,
    chopped coarsely
400g dark eating chocolate,
    chopped coarsely
peppermint oil or essence

1 Grease 19cm x 29cm baking tin; line with baking parchment, extending paper 5cm over long sides.
2 Combine sugar, milk, glucose and butter in medium heavy-based saucepan; stir over heat, without boiling, until sugar dissolves. Bring to a boil; boil, stirring, about 4 minutes or until mixture becomes the colour of creamed honey and begins to catch on the base of the pan.
3 Remove pan from heat; quickly stir in marshmallows and 250g of the chocolate. Flavour mixture with oil or essence to taste. Spread mixture into tin.
4 Working quickly, melt remaining chocolate in small heatproof bowl over small saucepan of simmering water (see pg 116); spread chocolate over slice. Refrigerate choc-mint slice until set before cutting.

makes 36

glazed almond biscuits

1 cup (120g) ground almonds
1 cup (160g) icing sugar
1 egg white
glaze
2 teaspoons gelatine
2 teaspoons caster sugar
¼ cup (60ml) boiling water

1 Grease two oven trays; line with baking parchment.
2 Combine ground almonds, sifted icing sugar and egg white in small bowl. Spoon mixture into piping bag fitted with 1cm-fluted tube.
3 Pipe shapes onto trays. Stand, uncovered, overnight to dry.
4 Preheat oven to 200°C/180°C fan-assisted. Bake biscuits, uncovered, about 5 minutes or until browned lightly.
5 Meanwhile, make glaze.
6 Cool biscuits for 1 minute on trays; transfer to wire rack. Brush hot biscuits with hot glaze; cool.
glaze Combine ingredients in small jug; stir until sugar and gelatine dissolve.

makes 40

fruit mince slice

90g butter, softened
⅓ cup (75g) firmly packed
   brown sugar
1 cup (150g) plain flour
icing sugar, for dusting
topping
1 cup (340g) fruit mincemeat
2 eggs
½ cup (110g) firmly packed
   brown sugar
2 tablespoons brandy
1 tablespoon self-raising flour
1½ cups (120g) desiccated
   coconut

1 Preheat oven to 180°C/160°C fan-assisted. Grease 20cm x 30cm baking tin; line with baking parchment, extending paper 5cm over long sides.
2 Beat butter and sugar in small bowl with electric mixer until pale in colour; stir in sifted flour, in two batches. Press dough over base of tin. Bake 10 minutes.
3 Meanwhile, make topping.
4 Press topping gently over base. Bake about 25 minutes or until slice is firm and golden brown. Cool slice in tin before cutting.
topping Blend or process fruit mince until chopped finely. Beat eggs, sugar and brandy in small bowl with electric mixer until thick and creamy; fold in flour, coconut and mincemeat.

makes 60

choccy orange sticks

2 large thick-skinned
   oranges (600g)
1 cup (220g) caster sugar
1 cup (250ml) water
200g dark eating chocolate,
   melted

1 Cut oranges into quarters. Peel away skin, leaving pith attached to skin. Cut skin with pith into 1cm-thick strips; discard fruit.
2 Drop orange strips into pan of boiling water, return to a boil; drain. Repeat twice.
3 Combine sugar and the water in medium saucepan. Stir over heat, without boiling, until sugar dissolves. Add strips; bring to a boil. Reduce heat; simmer, uncovered, stirring occasionally, about 5 minutes or until strips become translucent.
4 Meanwhile, place wire rack over baking-parchment-lined tray.
5 Remove strips from syrup with tongs; place on wire rack in single layer. Dry, uncovered, overnight.
6 Line tray with baking parchment. Using dipping forks (see pg 115), dip strips, one at a time, into chocolate; place on tray. Set at room temperature.

makes 48

chocolate marzipan almonds

30 (40g) whole blanched
  almonds
200g marzipan or almond paste
125g dark eating
  chocolate, melted

1 Preheat oven to 180°C/160°C fan-assisted.
2 Roast nuts in single layer on oven tray about 5 minutes or until golden brown; cool.
3 Mould level teaspoons of paste around each nut. Place on wire rack; stand, uncovered, overnight, until dry to touch.
4 Using dipping forks, dip each nut into chocolate (see pg 117). Place nuts on foil-lined tray; set at room temperature.

makes 30

cherry jubilee jellies

2 tablespoons gelatine
¾ cup (180ml) water
2 cups (440g) caster sugar
¾ cup (180ml) water, extra
2 tablespoons cherry brandy

1 Sprinkle gelatine over the water in small jug; stand about 5 minutes or until softened.
2 Meanwhile, combine sugar and the extra water in medium saucepan; stir over heat, without boiling, until sugar dissolves. Reduce heat; simmer, uncovered, about 10 minutes or until syrup is thicker, but still clear. Add gelatine mixture, stir until dissolved, then stir in brandy. Stand 10 minutes; skim any scum from surface.
3 Pour mixture into wetted 8cm x 26cm cake tin; refrigerate jelly about 3 hours or until firm.
4 Turn jelly onto board; cut into squares with hot, wet knife.

makes 52

jammy spice drops

30g butter
1/3 cup (115g) golden syrup
1 cup (150g) plain flour
1/2 teaspoon bicarbonate of soda
1/4 teaspoon ground ginger
1/4 teaspoon ground cardamom
1/4 teaspoon ground cinnamon
1/4 teaspoon ground cloves
1/2 teaspoon cocoa powder
1 tablespoon milk
2 tablespoons finely chopped
    mixed peel
1/4 cup (80g) raspberry jam
60g dark eating chocolate,
    melted

1 Melt butter in small saucepan; add syrup, bring to a boil. Remove pan from heat; stand 10 minutes.
2 Stir in sifted dry ingredients, milk and peel. Cover; cool 2 hours.
3 Preheat oven to 180°C/ 160°C fan-assisted. Grease two oven trays.
4 Knead dough on surface dusted with a little extra flour until dough loses stickiness.
5 Roll dough between sheets of baking parchment to about 8mm thickness. Cut out rounds using 4cm-fluted round cutter. Place about 3cm apart on trays.
6 Using end of handle of wooden spoon, gently press hollows into each round; fill with 1/2 teaspoon jam.
7 Bake 10 minutes; cool on trays.
8 Spread flat-sides of biscuits with chocolate. Place biscuits, jam-side down, on foil-lined trays; set at room temperature.

makes 24

lemon coconut macaroons

3 egg whites
2 tablespoons caster sugar
1¼ cups (200g) icing sugar
½ cup (60g) ground almonds
½ cup (40g) desiccated coconut
1 tablespoon icing sugar, extra
lemon cream
300ml whipping cream
1 tablespoon icing sugar
1 teaspoon finely grated
   lemon rind

1 Preheat oven to 150°C/ 130°C fan-assisted. Grease four oven trays; line with baking parchment.
2 Beat egg whites in small bowl with electric mixer until soft peaks form. Add caster sugar; beat until sugar dissolves. Transfer mixture to large bowl. Fold in sifted icing sugar, ground almonds and coconut, in two batches.
3 Spoon mixture into large piping bag fitted with 1.5cm plain tube. Pipe 4cm rounds, about 2cm apart, onto trays.
4 Tap trays on bench to help macaroons spread slightly. Dust macaroons with extra sifted icing sugar; stand 15 minutes.
5 Meanwhile, make lemon cream.
6 Bake macaroons 20 minutes. Stand 5 minutes; transfer to wire rack to cool.
7 Sandwich macaroons with lemon cream just before serving.
lemon cream Beat cream, icing sugar and rind in small bowl with electric mixer until firm peaks form.

makes 24

cherry almond coconut slice

60g butter, softened
⅓ cup (75g) caster sugar
1 egg yolk
2 tablespoons self-raising flour
½ cup (75g) plain flour
⅔ cup (220g) cherry jam
1 tablespoon cherry brandy
⅓ cup (25g) flaked almonds
topping
2 eggs
¼ cup (55g) caster sugar
2 cups (160g)
    desiccated coconut

1 Preheat oven to 180°C/160°C fan-assisted. Grease 19cm x 29cm baking tin; line with baking parchment, extending paper 5cm over long sides.
2 Beat butter, sugar and egg yolk in small bowl with electric mixer until light and fluffy. Stir in sifted flours. Press mixture into tin; spread with combined jam and brandy.
3 Make topping.
4 Sprinkle topping over slice, then sprinkle topping with nuts; press down gently.
5 Bake about 30 minutes; cool in tin before cutting.
topping Beat eggs and sugar together with fork in medium bowl; stir in coconut.

makes 54

AOMORI-SHI AOMORI
11-1KAMIKOBUNATO HANAMAKI SHI
2-3-12MAEGATA MORIOKA SHI IWATE
KITAKAMI-SHI IWATE
SHIBATA-GUN MIYAGI
UNIQLO YORKTOWNICHINAZAKA
WAKABAYASHI-KU SENDAI-SHI
1-1AZAFUKUROHIGASHI OONODA TAIHAKU-KU
SENDAI-SHI MIYAGI
FURUKAWAMINAMI TOCHIKUKAKUSEIRI
UEMATSU NATORI-SHI
2FAEON AKITANAKASAN
AKITA-SHI AKITA

sugary cinnamon twists

1 sheet ready-rolled
   puff pastry, thawed
20g butter, melted
2 tablespoons raw sugar
½ teaspoon ground cinnamon

1 Preheat oven to 200°C/
180°C fan-assisted. Grease two
oven trays.
2 Brush pastry with butter;
sprinkle with combined sugar
and cinnamon. Cut pastry in half.
Turn one half over, sugar-side
down; place the other half,
sugar-side up, on top. Press
lightly to join layers. Cut pastry
into 1cm-wide strips; twist each
strip (see pg 119), then place
on trays.
3 Bake about 10 minutes or until
browned lightly and crisp;
transfer to wire rack to cool.

makes 25

If you would like to make your own delicious pastry cases, see the recipe for pastry in blueberry apple crumbles on page 103.

395g can sweetened
   condensed milk
2 tablespoons golden syrup
60g unsalted butter
24 x 4.5cm diameter baked
   pastry cases
1 large banana (230g)
½ cup (125ml) whipping
   cream, whipped

1 Combine condensed milk, syrup and butter in small heavy-based saucepan; stir over heat until smooth.
2 Bring mixture to a boil; boil, stirring, about 10 minutes or until mixture is thick and dark caramel in colour. Remove pan from heat; cool.
3 Fill pastry cases with caramel; top with a slice of banana, then a dollop of cream.

makes 24

banoffee tartlets

apple charlotte tartlets

If you would like to make your own delicious pastry cases, see the recipe for pastry in blueberry apple crumbles on page 103.

2 medium green apples (300g), peeled, cored
1 tablespoon caster sugar
1 tablespoon water
1 clove
½ teaspoon ground cinnamon
24 x 4.5cm diameter baked pastry cases
½ cup (125ml) whipping cream, whipped
2 tablespoons passionfruit pulp

1 Thinly slice apples; combine in small saucepan with sugar, the water, clove and cinnamon; cover. Bring to a boil; reduce heat, simmer, covered, about 5 minutes or until apple softens.
2 Drain apple mixture; discard liquid and clove. Cool apple.
3 Place pastry cases on tray, fill with cold stewed apple; refrigerate 30 minutes.
4 Just before serving, top with cream, then drizzle with passionfruit pulp.

makes 24

If you would like to make your own delicious pastry cases, see the recipe for pastry in blueberry apple crumbles on page 103.

4 egg yolks
⅓ cup (75g) caster sugar
2 teaspoons finely
    grated lemon rind
¼ cup (60ml) lemon juice
40g unsalted butter, chopped
24 x 4.5cm diameter baked
    pastry cases
meringue
1 egg white
¼ cup (55g) caster sugar

1 Combine egg yolks, sugar, rind, juice and butter in small heatproof bowl; stir over small saucepan of simmering water until mixture thickens slightly and coats the back of a spoon. Remove pan from heat, remove bowl from pan immediately; cover surface of lemon curd with cling film; chill until cold.
2 Preheat oven to 200°C/180°C fan-assisted.
3 Meanwhile, make meringue.
4 Place pastry cases on oven tray; fill with curd, then top with meringue.
5 Bake about 5 minutes or until meringue is browned lightly.
meringue   Beat egg white in small bowl with electric mixer until soft peaks form; gradually add sugar, beating until dissolved between additions.

makes 24

lemon meringue tartlets

creamy caramels

1 cup (220g) caster sugar
90g unsalted butter
2 tablespoons golden syrup
⅓ cup (115g) glucose syrup
½ cup (125ml) sweetened
   condensed milk

1 Grease deep 19cm-square cake tin.
2 Combine sugar, butter, syrups, and milk in medium heavy-based saucepan; stir over heat, without boiling, until sugar is dissolved.
3 Bring to a boil; boil, stirring, about 7 minutes or until mixture is a caramel colour. Allow bubbles to subside; pour into tin, stand 10 minutes.
4 Mark squares using greased metal spatula (see pg 121). Cool before cutting.

makes 81

oaty bites

½ cup (45g) rolled oats
60g butter
1 tablespoon golden syrup
¼ teaspoon bicarbonate of soda
½ cup (75g) plain flour
½ cup (110g) caster sugar
⅓ cup (25g) desiccated coconut

1 Preheat oven to 150°C/ 130°C fan-assisted. Grease two oven trays.
2 Blend or process oats until chopped coarsely.
3 Combine butter and syrup in medium saucepan; stir over low heat until smooth. Remove pan from heat; stir in soda, then remaining ingredients.
4 Roll rounded teaspoons of the mixture into balls. Place about 5cm apart on trays; flatten slightly. Bake about 15 minutes; cool on trays.

makes 36

coconut ice

5¼ cups (840g) icing sugar
2½ cups (200g) desiccated
  coconut
395g can sweetened
  condensed milk
1 egg white, beaten lightly
pink food colouring

1 Line deep 19cm-square cake tin with strips of baking parchment.
2 Sift icing sugar into large bowl; stir in coconut, then condensed milk and egg white.
3 Divide mixture in half; tint half with pink colouring. Press pink mixture into tin then top with white mixture. Cover; refrigerate about 3 hours or until set before cutting into squares.

makes 64

lime and berry muffins

3 egg whites
90g unsalted butter, melted
1 teaspoon finely grated
   lime rind
½ cup (60g) ground almonds
¾ cup (120g) icing sugar
¼ cup (35g) plain flour
⅓ cup (50g) frozen blueberries
1 tablespoon icing sugar, extra

1 Preheat oven to 180°C/160°C fan-assisted. Grease two 12-hole (1-tablespoon/20ml) mini muffin trays.
2 Place egg whites in medium bowl, whisk until frothy. Stir in butter, rind, ground almonds and sifted icing sugar and flour.
3 Drop heaped teaspoons of mixture into each muffin tray hole; top each with a blueberry.
4 Bake about 10 minutes. Stand muffins in tray 5 minutes; turn onto wire rack to cool.
5 Dust with the sifted extra icing sugar.

makes 24

brandy snaps with hazelnut cream

This recipe makes a lot of tiny baskets; make as many as you need, then make the remaining mixture into larger snaps – serve them stacked, layered with cream for an easy dessert.

1 tablespoon golden syrup
30g butter
1½ tablespoons brown sugar
1½ tablespoons plain flour
1 teaspoon ground ginger
45 (⅓ cup) roasted hazelnuts
hazelnut cream
¾ cup (180ml) whipping cream
1 tablespoon hazelnut-flavoured
  liqueur

1 Preheat oven to 180°C/ 160°C fan-assisted. Grease two oven trays.
2 Combine syrup, butter and sugar in small saucepan; stir over low heat until smooth. Remove pan from heat; stir in sifted flour and ginger.
3 Drop four level ¼-teaspoons of mixture, about 5cm apart, on oven tray (for easier handling, bake only four at a time).
4 Bake about 4 minutes or until golden brown. Remove from oven; cool on tray 30 seconds. With rounded knife or metal spatula, quickly lift brandy snap from tray (see pg 125); shape each brandy snap into a basket-shape using an upturned foil petit-four case as a guide (see pg 125). Repeat with remaining mixture.

5 Make hazelnut cream.
6 Just before serving, fill baskets with hazelnut cream; top each with a nut.
hazelnut cream Beat cream and liqueur in small bowl with electric mixer until firm peaks form.

makes 45

choc-topped zucotto

2 eggs
⅓ cup (75g) caster sugar
2 tablespoons cornflour
2 tablespoons plain flour
2 tablespoons self-raising flour
200g milk eating chocolate
2 tablespoons icing sugar
nutty cream
½ cup (125ml) whipping cream
1 tablespoon icing sugar
1 tablespoon hazelnut-flavoured
 liqueur
2 tablespoons finely chopped
 roasted hazelnuts
2 tablespoons finely chopped
 roasted almonds

1 Preheat oven to 180°C/160°C fan-assisted. Grease and flour three 12-hole shallow round-based bun trays (see pg 115).
2 Beat eggs in small bowl with electric mixer until thick and creamy. Gradually add caster sugar, beating until sugar dissolves between additions. Sift flours together three times; fold into egg mixture.
3 Drop rounded tablespoons of mixture into trays. Bake about 7 minutes; turn onto wire racks to cool.
4 Meanwhile, coarsely grate 1 tablespoon of chocolate from the 200g block; reserve grated chocolate. Melt remaining chocolate (see pg 116).
5 Make nutty cream.

6 Dip the knuckle of your index finger into icing sugar then use to make a large hollow in the flat side of the cakes (see pg 123).
7 Spoon 1 teaspoon of the nutty cream into each hollow; smooth level. Spread with melted chocolate. Set at room temperature.
8 Dust zucotto with sifted icing sugar to serve.
nutty cream Beat cream, sifted icing sugar and liqueur in small bowl with electric mixer until firm peaks form. Stir in nuts and reserved grated chocolate.

makes 36

1 egg white
⅓ cup (55g) icing sugar
½ teaspoon vanilla extract
30g butter, melted
¼ cup (30g) ground almonds
¼ cup (35g) plain flour
filling
⅓ cup (50g) finely
   chopped raisins
¼ cup (60ml) dark rum
1 cinnamon stick
1 cup (240g) ricotta cheese
2 tablespoons honey

1 Preheat oven to 200°C/180°C fan-assisted. Grease two oven trays. Mark two 6cm-circles on each tray.
2 Beat egg white, sifted icing sugar and extract in small bowl with fork until foamy. Beat in butter, almonds and sifted flour.
3 Drop level teaspoons of mixture into circles, spread to fill circles. Bake about 4 minutes or until edges of cornettes are browned lightly (bake two cornettes at a time; they must be shaped quickly).
4 Using metal spatula, quickly lift one cornette from tray, roll into cone shape; hold gently until crisp (see pg 123). Repeat with remaining mixture.

5 Make filling.
6 Spoon filling into piping bag fitted with 1cm plain tube. Pipe mixture into cornettes.
filling Combine raisins, rum and cinnamon in small saucepan, stir over low heat until warm; cool then discard cinnamon. Combine cheese and honey in small bowl; stir in raisin mixture.

makes 20

rum & raisin cornettes

jewelettes

½ cup (70g) roasted
  unsalted pistachios
¼ cup (50g) halved green
  glacé cherries
¼ cup (50g) halved red
  glacé cherries
¼ cup (60g) coarsely chopped
  glacé peaches
¼ cup (55g) coarsely chopped
  stem ginger
200g white eating
  chocolate, melted

1 Grease 8cm x 26cm baking tin;
line base with baking parchment,
extending paper 5cm over
long sides.
2 Combine nuts, fruits and ginger
in medium bowl. Working quickly,
stir in chocolate; spread mixture
into tin, push down firmly to
flatten. Refrigerate until set.
3 Turn bar onto board, cut
into slices.

makes 16

pistachio almond crisps

3 egg whites
½ cup (110g) caster sugar
pinch ground cardamom
1 cup (150g) plain flour
½ cup (80g) blanched almonds
½ cup (70g) roasted
   unsalted pistachios

1 Preheat oven to 160°C/140°C fan-assisted. Grease 30cm-square piece of foil.

2 Beat egg whites in small bowl with electric mixer until soft peaks form. Gradually add sugar, beating until dissolved between additions. Transfer mixture to medium bowl.

3 Fold in sifted dry ingredients and nuts; spoon mixture onto foil, shape into 7cm x 25cm log. Enclose firmly in foil; place on oven tray.

4 Bake about 45 minutes or until firm. Turn log out of foil onto wire rack to cool.

5 Preheat oven temperature to 120°C/100°C fan-assisted.

6 Using serrated knife, slice log thinly. Place slices close together in single layer on oven trays. Bake about 20 minutes or until crisp; transfer to wire racks to cool. Store in airtight container at room temperature for up to four weeks.

makes 65

coconut ice-cream truffles

250ml vanilla ice-cream
2 teaspoons coconut-flavoured
   liqueur
1 tablespoon shredded coconut
125g plain sweet biscuits,
   crushed
400g white eating
   chocolate, melted
1¾ cups (135g) shredded
   coconut, extra

1 Combine slightly softened ice-cream, liqueur, coconut and biscuit in medium bowl. Cover with foil; freeze about 1 hour or until firm.
2 Working quickly, roll ½ level teaspoons of mixture into balls. Place on tray; freeze until firm.
3 Dip balls in melted chocolate (see pg 116); roll in extra coconut. Return to tray; freeze until firm.

makes 50

hazelnut Replace liqueur with 1 tablespoon chocolate hazelnut spread. Omit shredded coconut. Replace white chocolate with milk chocolate. Replace extra shredded coconut with 1½ cups finely chopped roasted hazelnuts.
mocha walnut Replace liqueur with 1 tablespoon strong black coffee. Omit shredded coconut. Replace white chocolate with dark chocolate. Replace extra shredded coconut with 1½ cups finely chopped roasted walnuts.

Coconut ice-cream truffles and mocha walnut ice-cream truffles

almond honey nougat

It is important to use a sugar thermometer in this recipe (see pg 120) in order to get the correct consistency when making the nougat.

Rice paper, used for confectionery, can be found in specialist food stores and some delicatessens.

2 sheets rice paper
½ cup (180g) honey
1⅓ cups (290g) caster sugar
2 tablespoons water
1 egg white
2 cups (320g) blanched
   almonds, roasted

1 Grease deep 15cm-square cake tin. Trim one sheet of rice paper to fit base of tin.
2 Combine honey, sugar and the water in small heavy-based saucepan with pouring lip; stir over heat, without boiling, until sugar dissolves. Bring to a boil; boil, without stirring, about 10 minutes or until syrup reaches 164°C on the sugar thermometer; remove pan from heat immediately. Remove thermometer from pan.
3 Beat egg white in small heatproof bowl with electric mixer until soft peaks form. With motor operating, add hot syrup to egg white in thin, steady stream.

4 Stir nuts into egg white mixture; spoon into tin. Press mixture firmly into tin. Cut remaining sheet of rice paper large enough to cover top of nougat; press gently onto nougat. Stand at room temperature about 2 hours or until cool.
5 Cut nougat into squares. Store in airtight container at room temperature.

makes 49

rosewater pistachio crêpes

½ cup (75g) plain flour
1 tablespoon caster sugar
2 eggs
¾ cup (180ml) milk
1 tablespoon vegetable oil
¼ cup (35g) finely chopped
    roasted unsalted pistachios
rosewater cream
⅔ cup (160ml) whipping cream
2 teaspoons icing sugar
½ teaspoon rosewater
pink food colouring

1 Sift flour and sugar into medium bowl, gradually stir in combined eggs, milk and oil; stir until smooth. Cover, stand 30 minutes.
2 Meanwhile, make rosewater cream.
3 Heat greased large heavy-based frying pan; pour ⅓ cup batter into pan, tilting pan to coat base evenly with batter.
4 Cook over low heat, loosening edge with spatula, until browned lightly. Turn crêpe; brown other side. Remove from pan. Repeat with remaining batter to make 4 crêpes. Using 6cm-fluted round cutter, cut 8 rounds from each crêpe.

5 Spoon rosewater cream into piping bag fitted with 1cm plain tube. Pipe cream in centre of each round; pinch middle of crêpes together to join.
6 Dip ends of each filled crêpe into nuts.

rosewater cream Beat cream, icing sugar and rosewater in small bowl with electric mixer until firm peaks form; tint pink with colouring.

makes 32

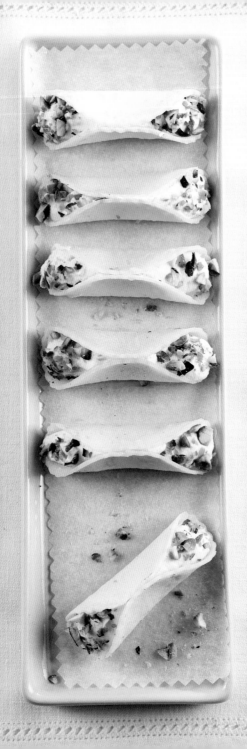

P E T I T S

honey ginger crunchies

25g butter
1 tablespoon honey
1½ cups (60g) cornflakes
¼ cup (20g) flaked almonds,
   roasted
¼ cup (55g) finely chopped
   glacé ginger

1 Preheat oven to 180°C/160°C fan-assisted. Line two 12-hole (1-tablespoon/20ml) mini muffin trays with foil cases.
2 Melt butter with honey in small saucepan. Combine butter mixture with cornflakes, nuts and ginger in large bowl.
3 Drop level tablespoons of mixture into each case. Bake about 10 minutes or until golden. Cool in trays.

makes 24

This mixture will make 2 cups mousse; divide it among small glasses for serving. 40ml shot glasses will give you about 12 delicious mini servings.

30g butter
120g white eating chocolate
2 egg whites
⅔ cup (160ml) whipping cream, whipped
green food colouring
2 teaspoons mint-flavoured liqueur

1 Melt butter in small saucepan or in microwave oven; stand 2 minutes. Skim off and reserve clarified butter from the top, leaving milky solids; discard solids.
2 Melt chocolate in medium heatproof bowl (see pg 116); stir in clarified butter.
3 Beat egg whites in small bowl with electric mixer until soft peaks form. Gently fold egg white, cream and colouring into white chocolate mixture; stir in liqueur.
4 Divide mousse among serving glasses; refrigerate about 3 hours or overnight.
5 Decorate mousse with sliced strawberries and fresh mint leaves, if you like.

serves 12

minted white chocolate mousse

brandied cream cheese prunes

24 large prunes with stones
1 tablespoon brandy
125g cream cheese, softened
2 tablespoons icing sugar
1 tablespoon roasted flaked
    almonds, chopped coarsely
50g white eating chocolate,
    melted

1 Make a shallow cut lengthways in each prune (do not cut all the way through); remove stones. Combine prunes and brandy in medium bowl; stand 15 minutes.
2 Meanwhile, combine cream cheese and sifted icing sugar in small bowl with wooden spoon; stir in nuts.
3 Drain brandy from prunes into cream cheese mixture; stir until combined. Place prunes on wire rack. Spoon cream cheese mixture into piping bag; pipe mixture into prunes (see pg 123).
4 Drizzle prunes with melted chocolate (see pg 116); set at room temperature.

makes 24

choc-orange ricotta dates

10 large fresh dates
1 tablespoon orange-flavoured
   liqueur
½ cup (120g) ricotta cheese
1 tablespoon icing sugar
1 teaspoon finely grated
   orange rind
50g dark eating
   chocolate, melted

1 Make a shallow cut lengthways in each date (do not cut all the way through); remove stones. Combine dates and liqueur in medium bowl; stand 15 minutes.
2 Meanwhile, combine cheese, sifted icing sugar and rind in small bowl with wooden spoon.
3 Drain liqueur from dates into cream cheese mixture; stir until combined. Place dates on wire rack. Spoon cream cheese mixture into piping bag; pipe mixture into dates (see pg 123).
4 Drizzle dates with melted chocolate (see pg 116); set at room temperature.

makes 10

Store marshmallows in an airtight container at room temperature for up to two weeks.

2 tablespoons (28g) gelatine
½ cup (125ml) cold water
2 cups (440g) caster sugar
1 cup (250ml) hot water
1 teaspoon rosewater
pink food colouring
1 cup (80g) desiccated coconut
¼ cup (20g) shredded coconut

1 Grease 25cm x 30cm swiss roll tin.
2 Sprinkle gelatine over the cold water in small bowl.
3 Combine sugar and the hot water in medium saucepan, stir over heat until sugar dissolves; bring to a boil. Add in gelatine mixture; boil, without stirring, 20 minutes. Cool to lukewarm.
4 Beat sugar mixture, flavouring and colouring in large bowl with electric mixer, on high speed, about 5 minutes or until mixture is thick and holds its shape.
5 Spread marshmallow mixture into swiss roll tin. Sprinkle marshmallow with a little of the combined coconut to cover top evenly. Set at room temperature for about 2 hours or until firm.
6 Cut marshmallow into squares.

makes 105

variations

orange Instead of the rosewater and pink food colouring, flavour the mixture with 1 teaspoon orange blossom water and tint with orange food colouring.
mint Instead of the rosewater and pink food colouring, flavour with ½ teaspoon peppermint essence or a few drops of peppermint oil and tint with green food colouring.

pink marshmallows

palmiers with honey cream

2 tablespoons raw sugar
1 sheet ready-rolled puff pastry
1 teaspoon ground nutmeg
300ml whipping cream
2 teaspoons honey

1 Preheat oven to 180°C/160°C fan-assisted. Grease two oven trays; line with baking parchment.

2 Sprinkle board lightly with a little of the sugar. Roll pastry on sugared board into 20cm x 40cm rectangle; trim edges. Sprinkle pastry with nutmeg and remaining sugar.

3 Starting from long side, loosely roll one side at a time into the middle of the rectangle, so the two long sides meet (see pg 118).

4 Cut pastry into 5mm-thick pieces. Place, cut-side up, about 5cm apart, on trays. Spread pastry open slightly at folded ends to make a V-shape (see pg 118).

5 Bake palmiers about 15 minutes or until golden brown; transfer to wire rack to cool.

6 Beat cream and honey in small bowl with electric mixer until firm peaks form. Serve palmiers with honey cream.

makes 30

lemon shortbread

We found the combination of regular table (salted) butter with unsalted butter gave the yummiest results.

60g unsalted butter, softened
60g butter, softened
2 teaspoons finely grated
  lemon rind
2 tablespoons caster sugar
1 cup (150g) plain flour
2 tablespoons rice flour
1 tablespoon demerara sugar

1 Preheat oven to 160°C/ 140°C fan-assisted. Grease two oven trays.
2 Beat butters, rind and caster sugar in small bowl with electric mixer until light and fluffy.
3 Stir in sifted flours in two batches. Turn dough onto floured surface, knead dough for 5 minutes.
4 Roll dough between sheets of baking parchment until 5mm thick. Using 5cm star-shaped cutter, cut out stars. Place about 3cm apart on trays.
5 Sprinkle stars with demerara sugar. Bake about 10 minutes; transfer to wire racks to cool.

makes 15

butteryscotch

2 cups (440g) caster sugar
⅓ cup (80ml) water
⅔ cup (230g) glucose syrup
125g unsalted butter, chopped

1 Grease 19cm x 29cm baking tin; line base with baking parchment, extending paper 5cm over long sides.
2 Combine sugar, the water and glucose in medium heavy-based saucepan; stir over heat, without boiling, until sugar is dissolved. Bring to a boil; boil, uncovered, about 15 minutes or until mixture is golden brown (150°C on a sugar thermometer, see pg 120).
3 Remove pan from heat; allow bubbles to subside. Add butter; stir gently until smooth. Pour into baking tin; stand 10 minutes. Using greased metal spatula, mark butterscotch into squares (see pg 121).
4 Cool butterscotch at room temperature. When cold, break into pieces.

makes 150

1½ cups (330g) caster sugar
½ cup (125ml) water
2 teaspoons glucose syrup
15g butter
1 tablespoon rum
¾ cup (120g) brazil nuts

1 Combine sugar, the water and glucose in large heavy-based saucepan; stir over heat, without boiling, until sugar is dissolved. Bring to a boil; boil about 20 minutes or until a teaspoon of hot toffee will set and crack when dropped into a cup of cold water.

2 Meanwhile, line oven trays with baking parchment.

3 Remove pan from heat, allow bubbles to subside; add butter and rum, stir gently. Add nuts; tilt pan until nuts are well coated in toffee mixture.

4 Working quickly, using greased tongs or two forks, lift nuts, one at a time, out of toffee; place on tray, set at room temperature.

makes 40

buttered rum brazil nuts

coconut squares

We've used shredded coconut in our picture, but feel free to mix and match using shredded, desiccated or flaked. If you use flaked coconut, be sure to blend or process it until it's chopped coarsely; this helps it to stick to the icing.

90g butter, softened
½ teaspoon vanilla extract
½ cup (110g) caster sugar
2 eggs
1 cup (150g) self-raising flour
2 tablespoons milk
2¼ cups (180g) shredded
 coconut
chocolate icing
2 cups (320g) icing sugar
¼ cup (25g) cocoa powder
10g butter
½ cup (125ml) milk

1 Preheat oven to 180°C/160°C fan-assisted. Grease 19cm x 29cm baking tin; line with baking parchment.
2 Beat butter, extract, sugar, eggs, flour and milk in small bowl with electric mixer on low speed until ingredients are combined. Increase speed to medium; beat until mixture is pale in colour. Spread mixture evenly into tin.
3 Bake cake about 20 minutes. Stand 5 minutes; turn onto wire rack to cool. Cover with cling film; stand overnight.
4 Trim top and sides from cake to make cake a 18cm x 28cm rectangle. Cut cake into 2cm squares. Freeze squares about 30 minutes before dipping in icing.
5 Make chocolate icing.

6 Place coconut in small bowl. Hold each cake on a bamboo skewer, dip into icing; hold over bowl to drain excess icing.
7 Toss cakes, one at a time, in coconut. Stand squares on wire rack until set.
chocolate icing Sift icing sugar and cocoa into medium heatproof bowl; stir in butter and milk. Stand bowl over hot water; stir until icing is of a good coating consistency. As icing thickens, add a little hot water to bring it back to the correct consistency.

makes 126

coffee meringue kisses

¾ cup (165g) caster sugar
1 teaspoon instant
   coffee granules
¼ cup (60ml) water
1 egg white
1 teaspoon malt vinegar
2 teaspoons cornflour
coffee butter cream
1 teaspoon instant
   coffee granules
2 teaspoons hot water
2 teaspoons coffee-flavoured
   liqueur
60g unsalted butter, softened
⅔ cup (110g) icing sugar

1 Preheat oven to 120°C/100°C fan-assisted. Grease four oven trays; line with baking parchment.
2 Combine sugar, coffee and the water in small saucepan; stir over heat until sugar is dissolved. Bring to a boil; remove pan from heat.
3 Meanwhile, combine egg white, vinegar and cornflour in small heatproof bowl; beat with electric mixer until foamy. With motor operating, add hot syrup to egg white in a thin, steady stream; beat about 10 minutes or until mixture is thick.

4 Spoon meringue into piping bag fitted with 5mm-fluted tube; pipe meringues, about 2.5cm in diameter, about 3cm apart, on trays. Bake about 30 minutes or until dry to touch. Cool on trays.
5 Meanwhile, make coffee butter cream. Sandwich meringues with butter cream just before serving.
coffee butter cream Dissolve coffee in the water; add liqueur. Beat butter and sifted icing sugar until light and fluffy; beat in coffee mixture.

makes 45

strawberry powder puffs

2 eggs
⅓ cup (75g) caster sugar
2 tablespoons cornflour
2 tablespoons plain flour
2 tablespoons self-raising flour
½ cup (125ml) whipping cream
2 tablespoons icing sugar
½ cup (65g) finely
   chopped strawberries

1 Preheat oven to 180°C/160°C fan-assisted. Grease and flour two 12-hole shallow round-based bun trays.
2 Beat eggs and sugar in small bowl with electric mixer about four minutes or until thick and creamy.
3 Meanwhile, triple-sift flours; fold into egg mixture.
4 Drop 1 teaspoon of mixture into holes of trays. Bake about 7 minutes; turn immediately onto wire racks to cool. Wash, grease and flour trays again; continue using mixture until all puffs are baked.
5 Beat cream and half the sifted icing sugar in small bowl with electric mixer until firm peaks form; fold in strawberries.
6 Sandwich puffs with strawberry cream just before serving. Dust with remaining sifted icing sugar.

makes 36

¼ cup (60ml) water
30g butter
¼ cup (35g) plain flour
1 egg, beaten lightly
1 tablespoon icing sugar
coffee liqueur cream
⅔ cup (160ml) whipping cream
1 tablespoon icing sugar
1 tablespoon coffee-flavoured
   liqueur

1 Preheat oven to 200°C/180°C fan-assisted. Lightly grease two oven trays.
2 Combine the water and butter in small saucepan, bring to a boil; add sifted flour, stirring until mixture leaves side of pan. Remove pan from heat; cool 5 minutes.
3 Transfer mixture to small bowl; beat with electric mixer on medium speed. Gradually add egg, beating until mixture is glossy.
4 Spoon mixture into small piping bag fitted with 1.5cm plain tube. Pipe 2cm rounds, about 5cm apart, onto oven trays.
5 Bake 10 minutes. Reduce heat to 180°C/160°C fan-assisted; bake about 20 minutes or until puffs are crisp.

6 Remove puffs from oven; make small slits in sides of each puff to let steam escape. Transfer puffs to wire rack to cool.
7 Meanwhile, make coffee liqueur cream.
8 Just before serving, place coffee liqueur cream in small piping bag fitted with 4mm plain tube. Make small hole in bottom of each puff; pipe cream into puffs. Dust with sifted icing sugar.
coffee liqueur cream Beat cream, sifted icing sugar and liqueur in small bowl with electric mixer until firm peaks form.

makes 15

coffee liqueur puffs

little apricot macaroons

¼ cup (40g) finely chopped
  dried apricots
1 teaspoon orange-flavoured
  liqueur
1 egg white
¼ cup (55g) caster sugar
1 cup (75g) desiccated coconut
1 tablespoon finely chopped
  white eating chocolate

1 Preheat oven to 150°C/130°C fan-assisted. Line two 12-hole (1-tablespoon/20ml) mini muffin trays with paper cases.
2 Combine apricots and liqueur in small bowl.
3 Beat egg whites in another small bowl with electric mixer until soft peaks form; gradually add sugar, beating until dissolved between additions. Fold in apricot mixture, coconut and chocolate.
4 Place 1 heaped teaspoon in each paper case. Bake about 20 minutes; cool in trays.

makes 24

sienna discs

2 tablespoons caster sugar
¼ cup (90g) honey
⅓ cup (55g) blanched
   almonds, roasted
½ cup (70g) roasted hazelnuts
1 glacé apricot (30g)
1 glacé pineapple ring (30g)
2 tablespoons mixed peel
⅓ cup (50g) plain flour
1 tablespoon cocoa powder
½ teaspoon ground cinnamon
30g dark eating
   chocolate, melted
100g dark eating chocolate,
   melted, extra

1 Preheat oven to 160°C/140°C fan-assisted. Grease 40cm-long strip of foil.
2 Combine caster sugar and honey in small saucepan; stir over heat until sugar is dissolved. Bring to a simmer; simmer, without stirring, until syrup thickens slightly. Remove pan from heat.
3 Meanwhile, chop nuts, fruit and peel finely; combine mixture in medium bowl with syrup.
4 Stir in sifted flour, cocoa and cinnamon, then chocolate.
5 Shape mixture into 5cm-diameter log; roll tightly in foil, place on oven tray.
6 Bake 45 minutes; remove foil, cool on tray overnight.
7 Slice log; place slices on wire racks, pipe or drizzle extra chocolate over slices (see pg 116). Set at room temperature.

makes 30

peanut brittle pops

Using a saucepan with a pouring lip (see pg 115) makes it easy to pour the hot toffee into the trays.

3 cups (660g) caster sugar
1 cup (250ml) water
½ cup (70g) unsalted
   roasted peanuts
12 lolly sticks

1 Stir sugar and the water in medium heavy-based saucepan over heat until sugar dissolves. Bring to a boil; boil about 10 minutes or until toffee turns golden brown (see pg 120).
2 Remove pan from heat; allow bubbles to subside.
3 Meanwhile, divide nuts among two greased 12-hole (1-tablespoon/20ml) mini muffin trays. Cut lolly sticks in half.
4 Pour toffee slowly over nuts; cool pops about 10 minutes. Position a lolly stick, cut-side down, in each pop. Cool at room temperature.

makes 24

1 sheet ready-rolled puff pastry
¼ cup (55g) caster sugar
¼ cup (35g) cornflour
1½ tablespoons
   custard powder
1¼ cups (310ml) milk
30g butter
1 egg yolk
½ teaspoon vanilla extract
passionfruit icing
¾ cup (110g) icing sugar
1 tablespoon passionfruit pulp
1 teaspoon water,
   approximately

1 Preheat oven to 240°C/220°C fan-assisted. Grease 8cm x 26cm baking tin; line with strip of foil extending over long sides of tin.
2 Place pastry sheet on oven tray. Bake about 15 minutes or until puffed; cool. Split pastry in half horizontally; remove and discard any uncooked pastry from centre. Flatten pastry pieces gently with hand; trim both to fit pan. Place top half in tin, top-side down.
3 Meanwhile, combine sugar, cornflour and custard powder in medium saucepan; gradually stir in milk. Stir over heat until mixture boils and thickens. Reduce heat; simmer, stirring, about 3 minutes or until custard is thick and smooth. Remove pan from heat; stir in butter, egg yolk and extract.

4 Spread hot custard over the pastry in tin; top with remaining pastry, bottom-side up, press down gently. Cool to room temperature.
5 Meanwhile, make passionfruit icing.
6 Spread pastry with icing; set at room temperature. Refrigerate 3 hours before cutting.
passionfruit icing Sift icing sugar into small heatproof bowl; stir in passionfruit and enough water to make a thick paste. Stir over small saucepan of simmering water until icing is spreadable.

makes 8

vanilla passionfruit slice

lemon madeleines

2 eggs
2 tablespoons caster sugar
2 tablespoons icing sugar
2 teaspoons finely
   grated lemon rind
¼ cup (35g) self-raising flour
¼ cup (35g) plain flour
75g unsalted butter, melted
1 tablespoon lemon juice
2 tablespoons icing sugar, extra

1 Preheat oven to 200°C/
180°C fan-assisted. Grease
12-hole (1½-tablespoons/30ml)
madeleine tin.
2 Beat eggs, caster sugar, sifted
icing sugar and rind in small bowl
with electric mixer until pale
and thick.
3 Meanwhile, triple-sift flours;
sift flour over egg mixture. Pour
butter and juice down the side
of the bowl then fold ingredients
together.
4 Drop rounded tablespoons
of mixture into each hole of tin.
Bake about 10 minutes. Tap hot
tin firmly on bench to release
madeleines onto wire rack
to cool.
5 Dust with sifted extra icing
sugar to serve.

makes 12

blueberry apple crumbles

1 cup (150g) plain flour
⅓ cup (55g) icing sugar
90g unsalted butter, chopped
1 egg yolk
3 teaspoons iced water,
  approximately
2 tablespoons roasted
  slivered almonds
filling
1 small apple (130g),
  grated coarsely
½ cup (75g) frozen blueberries
1 teaspoon ground cinnamon
2 teaspoons finely grated
  lemon rind

1 Preheat oven to 180°C/160°C
fan-assisted. Grease two 12-hole
(1-tablespoon/20ml) mini
muffin trays.
2 Pulse sifted flour, sugar and
butter in food processor until
crumbly. Add egg yolk and
enough of the water to make
mixture come together.
3 Shape one-quarter of the
dough into thick sausage; wrap
in cling film, freeze 45 minutes.
4 Meanwhile, roll remaining
dough to 4mm thickness, cut out
6cm rounds (see pg 119); press
dough into holes of muffin
tray (see pg 119). Refrigerate
15 minutes.
5 Make filling; divide filling among
pastry cases.
6 Coarsely grate frozen dough
evenly over filling; sprinkle with
nuts. Bake about 20 minutes.
Stand 5 minutes; transfer to wire
rack to cool.
filling Combine apple, berries,
cinnamon and rind in small bowl.

makes 24

bumble bee liquorice

150g soft fondant icing
yellow food colouring
10 sticks soft liquorice (125g)
½ cup (80g) icing sugar

1 Tint 100g soft icing yellow by kneading food colouring into the icing on a surface dusted with sifted icing sugar. Knead remaining white icing until soft. Enclose icings in cling film until ready to use.
2 Roll pieces of liquorice firmly with rolling pin to about 3mm thickness (see pg 124).
3 Roll pieces of soft icing to the same thickness as liquorice pieces (see pg 124).
4 Stack the liquorice and icings, alternating colours (see pg 124).
5 Cut stack into 2cm pieces (see pg 125). Stand pieces on baking-parchment-lined tray until firm.

makes 20

toffeecomb with chocolate dip

It is important to use a sugar thermometer in this recipe (see pg 120) in order to get the correct consistency when making the toffee.

1 cup (220g) caster sugar
¼ cup (90g) golden syrup
1 tablespoon water
1 tablespoon bicarbonate
    of soda
125g dark eating
    chocolate, melted
2 tablespoons double cream

1 Grease 19cm x 29cm shallow cake tin.
2 Combine sugar, syrup and the water in medium heavy-based saucepan; stir over heat, without boiling, until sugar dissolves.
3 Place sugar thermometer in syrup, bring to a boil; boil about 5 minutes or until temperature reaches 148°C.
4 Remove pan from heat; immediately stir in soda.
5 Using metal spatula, quickly spread mixture into tin; cool at room temperature.
6 Break toffeecomb into pieces. Serve with combined chocolate and cream.

serves 10

1 cup (150g) self-raising flour
1 tablespoon caster sugar
1 egg
1¼ cups (310ml) buttermilk
25g unsalted butter, melted
½ cup (70g) fresh raspberries,
   chopped coarsely
½ cup (120g) crème fraîche
½ cup (70g) fresh raspberries,
   extra

1 Sift flour and sugar into medium bowl. Whisk egg, buttermilk and butter in medium jug.
2 Gradually whisk egg mixture into flour mixture until smooth. Stir in chopped raspberries. Transfer batter to jug.
3 Pour 1 tablespoon batter into heated greased large heavy-based frying pan for each pikelet. Cook pikelets until bubbles appear on the surface; turn each pikelet with metal spatula to brown lightly on the other side. Grease pan as needed during cooking. Cool pikelets on wire rack.
4 Serve pikelets topped with the crème fraîche and extra raspberries.

makes 30

raspberry pikelets with crème fraîche

chocolate peanut butter flowers

180g white eating chocolate,
   chopped coarsely
1 tablespoon smooth
   peanut butter
200g dark eating chocolate,
   chopped coarsely

1 Grease 25cm x 30cm swiss roll tin; line base with baking parchment, extending paper 5cm above long sides of tin.
2 Melt white chocolate in small heatproof bowl (see pg 116); stir in peanut butter.
3 Melt dark chocolate in another small heatproof bowl; cool 5 minutes.
4 Drop alternate tablespoonfuls of white chocolate mixture and dark chocolate into tin.
5 Gently shake tin to level mixture; pull a skewer backwards and forwards through mixture several times for a marbled effect. Stand at room temperature about 2 hours or until set.
6 Using 5cm flower cutter, cut out shapes; store in single layer in refrigerator.

makes 28

15 medium strawberries
1 tablespoon liqueur of your
choice, approximately
⅓ cup (80ml) double cream

1 Cut small slice from pointy-end of each strawberry so they stand upright. Cut tops off strawberries.
2 Using small pointed knife, hollow out strawberry centres.
3 Pour about ¼ teaspoon of liqueur into each strawberry.
4 Using teaspoon or small piping bag fitted with 1.5cm plain tube, pipe cream into strawberries. Position strawberry tops on cream.

makes 15

strawberry liqueur surprises

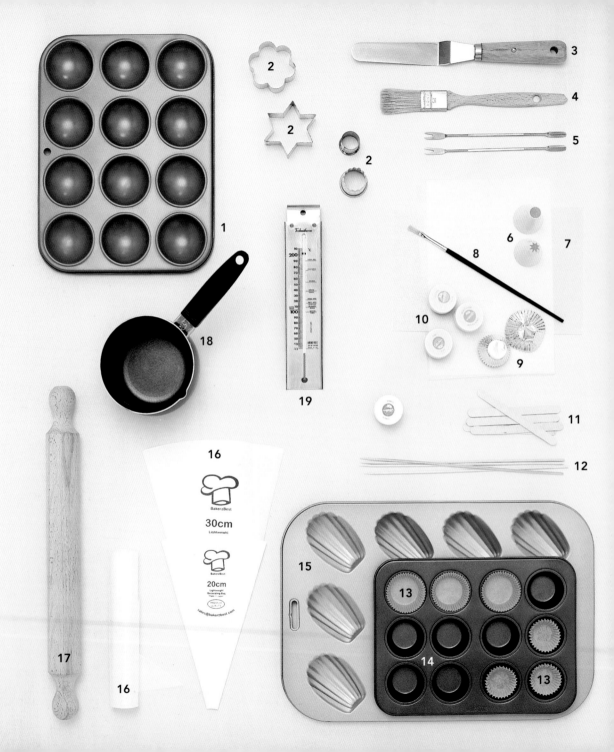

equipment

1. round-based bun trays
Available from supermarkets, chain stores and cookware shops, they are also called tartlet pans. They come in frames of 12, and can be made from aluminium or tin.

2. cutters
Come in all shapes and sizes, and are made from either plastic or metal. Can be bought from specialty cookware shops or cake decorating suppliers.

3. palette knife
The one pictured has a 'step', which is good for spreading icings, or there is also the plain bladed (straight) variety. Available from chain stores, supermarkets and cookware shops.

4. pastry brush
Come in handy not only for glazing various foods, but also for cleaning up around cakes.

5. dipping forks
Proper chocolate-dipping forks can be bought from specialty cookware shops, or you can buy the cheap similar versions pictured here, from chain stores.

6. piping tubes
Come in all shapes and sizes, both in metal and plastic; the best quality ones are available from chefs' suppliers and cake decorating suppliers.

7. baking parchment
We use baking parchment for lining cake tins and making paper piping bags.

8. artist's brush
A few different sized artist's brushes come in handy for things like brushing chocolate inside foil cases.

9. foil cases
These come in a variety of colours and many sizes and thicknesses, from the tiny petit four cases to large muffin size. Petit four cases are made from a strong, rigid foil. Supermarkets, chain stores and cookware shops carry these cases.

10. colourings
The quality and price of food colourings vary a lot. The more expensive colourings are highly concentrated, so will give more intense colours and will last longer than the more diluted, less expensive colourings.

11. lolly sticks
Used in craft and cooking; we've inserted them in toffee to make a handle for our peanut brittle pops.

12. bamboo skewers
Can be bought from supermarkets and Asian food stores. They come in handy for supporting cakes, as well as testing cakes to see if they are cooked through.

13. paper cake cases
Many coloured, patterned and different-sized cases are available in supermarkets and chain stores, but, if you want specific colours, you'll have to go to cake decorating suppliers.

14. mini muffin tray
Come in a frame consisting of 6, 12 or 24 holes; each hole has a 1-tablespoon capacity. They are available in supermarkets, chain stores and cookware shops.

15. madeleine tin
The traditional French madeleine cake, for which the tins were designed, is a light bite of sponge, best eaten fresh from the oven.

16. bought piping bags
Available from supermarkets, cookware shops and chain stores.

17. rolling pin
Come in wood, glass and various synthetic materials; all work well.

18. saucepan with pouring lip
Called milk saucepans; buy the heaviest-based saucepan you can if you're going to use it for making confectionery.

19. sugar thermometer
This should be a once-in-a-lifetime investment; keep it in a safe place, away from bumps, preferably wrapped in a tea-towel to protect the bulb from being broken.

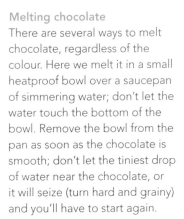

Melting chocolate

There are several ways to melt chocolate, regardless of the colour. Here we melt it in a small heatproof bowl over a saucepan of simmering water; don't let the water touch the bottom of the bowl. Remove the bowl from the pan as soon as the chocolate is smooth; don't let the tiniest drop of water near the chocolate, or it will seize (turn hard and grainy) and you'll have to start again.

Dipping ice-cream truffles

Make sure the ice-cream truffles are frozen solid before you start dipping. Work with only a few truffles at a time, keep the rest in the freezer, particularly if the kitchen is warm. Use two regular table forks, or even better, dipping forks (see pg 115). Dip the truffles, let the excess chocolate drain away, then roll in coating; place truffles on foil or baking parchment, return to the freezer to re-freeze.

Piping chocolate

Use a plastic or fabric piping bag (see pg 122) fitted with a fine plain piping tube, or a paper piping bag made from baking parchment (see pg 122). Half-fill the bag with melted chocolate. Use sharp scissors to snip a tiny piece from the tip of the paper bag to pipe through. If the hole is too small, continue to snip tiny pieces off until you can pipe the right thickness of chocolate.

chocolate

Dipping marzipan almonds
The chocolate should be at the stage where it has reached a good coating consistency, not too hot and not too cool; you might have to experiment with a couple of almonds to get the consistency just right. Using two table forks, or preferably dipping forks (see pg 115), work as quickly as you can dipping the almonds in and out of the chocolate. Drain off excess chocolate, then place onto a foil- or baking-parchment-lined tray to set at room temperature.

Choc-coating petit four cases
Use small foil petit four cases for this as they are quite strong and rigid enough to hold the chocolate. They come in many colours and are available at specialty cookware shops. Use an artist's brush (see pg 115) dipped in melted chocolate to brush a thick layer of chocolate evenly inside each foil case. These are at their best set at room temperature, but if you're in a hurry, refrigerate them.

Removing petit four cases
Once the chocolate cases have set, using your fingers, and handling the cases gently, ease away the foil cases from the chocolate; you'll be surprised how easy it is to do this. If the cases are refrigerator-cold, leave them to stand for about 10 minutes to let them come to room temperature, before removing the foil cases.

Folding pastry for palmiers (1)
Roll the sheet of thawed puff pastry on a sugared surface to 20cm x 40cm. Using a sharp knife, trim all four sides neatly, keeping the rectangular shape. Sprinkle the pastry evenly with sugar and nutmeg. Starting from a long side, loosely roll one side at a time into the middle of the rectangle, so the two long sides meet.

Folding pastry for palmiers (2)
Fold the long outside edges into the centre again. Turn the pastry piece on its side.

Preparing palmiers for baking
Use a sharp knife to cut each palmier about 5cm in thickness; put them, cut-side up, on a baking-paper-lined oven tray, about 5cm apart. Gently pull the pastry apart to make a V-shape, this will help shape the palmiers during baking.

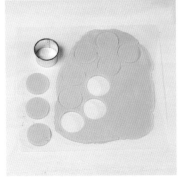

Shaping sugary cinnamon twists
Gently twist each strip of pastry by holding ends of each strip with fingers, and turning each end in a different direction; place twists about 5cm apart on baking-parchment-lined oven trays.

Handling pastry
Divide pastry in half, or quarters, depending on how much pastry you can handle at the one time, this pastry is quite soft. Roll chilled pastry between sheets of baking parchment to 4mm thickness. Using sharp 6cm cutter, cut out rounds from pastry.

Lining trays with pastry
Gently ease each round of pastry into each hole of the muffin tray; don't stretch the pastry. You'll get an even better result with this pastry if you refrigerate it for about 30 minutes before baking. This will help reduce shrinkage of the pastry and result in crisper pastry cases.

Handling sugar syrup

Use a heavy-based saucepan of the size we suggest, so that the correct amount of evaporation can take place. We indicate cooking times in our recipes, but they're only a guide. Stir the sugar and water over a medium to high heat until the sugar is dissolved, remove any sugar crystals on the side of the pan with a brush dipped in water.

Using a sugar thermometer

The correct way to use a thermometer is to place it in a small saucepan of cold water, bring it to the boil, check for accuracy then, when the syrup is boiling, transfer the thermometer into the syrup. After the correct temperature is reached, return the thermometer to the pan of boiling water, turn off the heat, and leave the thermometer to cool with the water.

Boiling sugar syrup

If we suggest you use a sugar thermometer, the temperature of the syrup will be critical for success. But, with basic toffees and caramels, you can easily get away with testing the syrup/toffee in water. After some practice, you'll recognise the colour that the sugar syrup should be.

Testing toffee or caramel

When you think the syrup has reached the colour we suggest, remove the pan from the heat, remembering that the syrup will continue to cook and darken during this time, so allow for this. Let the bubbles subside, then drop a teaspoon of the syrup into a cup of cold water.

Judging toffee

The toffee will set the instant it hits the cold water; lift it out and break it with your fingers. Taste a piece and, if you decide after this that the toffee needs to be a richer caramel flavour, or harder, then return the mixture to the heat and cook a little more. This test is easy, but a thermometer removes all the guess work for you.

Marking caramel

If you want a caramel to be cut into neat pieces, then it's vital that you mark the unset mixture before it sets. The right time to mark the caramel varies depending on the temperature reached. Grease the blade of a thin metal spatula or large knife, and, after the caramel has stood for about 10 minutes, start to mark a line in the caramel. If the line doesn't hold its shape, then wait a few more minutes. Mark the caramel all the way through to the base of the tin.

piping bags

Making a paper piping bag (1)
Cut a 25cm square from a sheet of baking parchment or greaseproof paper; fold the square in half diagonally then cut out the two triangles. With the apex of one triangle pointing towards you, hold the other two points, wrapping them around to form a cone.

Making a paper piping bag (2)
Bring the three points of the triangle together. Secure the bag with a staple if you're using baking parchment, or with sticky tape if you're using greaseproof paper. Half-fill the bag with icing etc, then, using sharp scissors, snip a tiny piece from the point of the bag for piping.

Ready-made piping bags
There are many types, shapes and sizes available. Rolls of plastic disposable piping bags are available from supermarkets, complete with various-shaped plastic piping tubes. Bags made from various types of fabrics are available from specialty cookware shops, and cake-decorator supplier shops.

Shaping zucottos

As soon as the baked zucottos are cool enough to handle, use the knuckle of your forefinger to gently push into the centre and shape each zucotto. Cool zucottos before filling.

Piping filling into prunes/dates

Using a piping bag only, pipe filling into prunes/dates, as shown. Piping is far more efficient, and neater, than trying to fill the prunes/dates using a teaspoon. Piping is easy, just practice a little by piping the filling onto baking parchment, then re-use it for filling the prunes/dates.

Shaping cornettes

As soon as the baked flat cornettes are cool enough to handle, and before they become crisp, quickly shape and pinch each cornette into a cone shape; hold gently until crisp. Cool on a wire rack.

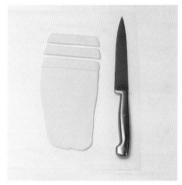

Rolling liquorice
Using a rolling pin (a small one is best, but not essential), roll each strip of soft liquorice on baking parchment until flattened to about 3mm in thickness.

Rolling soft icing
Using rolling pin, gently roll the icings on baking parchment or icing-sugared covered surface as evenly as possible, without rolling over the edges, into a flat piece about 3mm in thickness. Using a sharp knife, cut the icings into strips, the same length as the liquorice.

Stacking soft icing and liquorice
Stack the soft icings and the liquorice in any coloured layer combination you like.

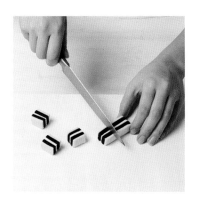

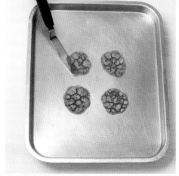

Cutting bumble-bee liquorice
Using sharp knife, cut the stack of liquorice and soft icing into bite-sized pieces; place on a baking-parchment-covered wire rack to dry. This will take from a few hours to overnight, depending on the weather. Store in an airtight container.

Removing brandy snap from tray
As soon as the snaps are ready to remove from the oven tray, you'll need to work quickly, as they will be beginning to firm and set as they cool. You will work out why we advise to only bake four snaps at the one time. Using a metal spatula, loosen one flat snap from the oven tray.

Shaping brandy snaps
Quickly shape the snap over the bottom of an upturned foil petit four case. If the remaining snaps are too firm to handle, return the tray to the oven for a minute to re-soften, you will become faster at shaping the baskets as you go along.

glossary

almonds
blanched brown skins removed.
flaked paper-thin slices.
ground also known as almond meal.
marzipan a paste made from ground almonds, sugar and water.
slivered small pieces cut lengthways.
baking powder a raising agent consisting mainly of two parts cream of tartar to one part bicarbonate of soda (baking soda).
bicarbonate of soda also known as baking soda.
cheese
cream also known as philadelphia; a soft, cow's-milk cheese.
ricotta soft, sweet, moist, white cow's-milk cheese with a low-fat content and a slightly grainy texture.
chocolate
dark eating made of cocoa liquor, cocoa butter and sugar.
milk eating most popular eating chocolate; mild and very sweet.
white eating contains no cocoa solids but derives its sweet flavour from cocoa butter. Very sensitive to heat.
cocoa powder also called cocoa; unsweetened, dried, roasted then ground cocoa beans.
coconut
desiccated unsweetened, dried, concentrated, shredded coconut.
flaked dried flaked coconut flesh.
shredded unsweetened thin strips of dried coconut flesh.
cornflakes commercially made cereal; dehydrated then baked crisp flakes of corn.

cornflour also known as cornstarch; available made from corn or wheat.
cream
double very rich, versatile cream; it withstands boiling, and whips and freezes well.
pouring also known as single cream.
whipping a cream for whipping.
cream of tartar the acid ingredient in baking powder; when added to confectionery mixtures it helps to prevent sugar crystallising.
crème fraîche a naturally fermented cream having a velvety texture and slightly tangy, nutty flavour.
custard powder instant mixture used to make pouring custard; similar to North American instant pudding mixes.
essence synthetically produced substances used in small amounts to impart their flavours to foods.
flour
plain also known as all-purpose.
rice very fine, gluten-free flour; made from ground white rice.
self-raising all-purpose plain flour with baking powder added in the proportion of 1 cup flour to 2 teaspoons baking powder.
food colouring vegetable-based substances; available in liquid, paste or gel form.
gelatine a thickening agent. We used powdered gelatine; is also available in sheets called leaf gelatine.
glacé fruit fruit cooked in heavy sugar syrup then dried.
glucose syrup also known as liquid glucose; made from wheat starch.

golden syrup a by-product of refined sugarcane; pure maple syrup or honey can be substituted.
liqueurs
cherry-flavoured use Kirsch or any generic brand.
coconut-flavoured use Malibu or any generic brand.
coffee-flavoured use Tia Maria, Kahlua or any generic brand.
hazelnut-flavoured use Frangelico or any generic brand.
mint-flavoured use Crème de Menthe or any generic brand.
orange-flavoured use Cointreau, Grand Marnier or any generic brand.
milk
buttermilk sold alongside fresh milk products in supermarkets and is commercially made by a method similar to yogurt.
evaporated unsweetened canned milk from which water has been extracted by evaporation.
sweetened condensed a canned milk product consisting of milk with more than half the water content removed and sugar added to the milk that remains.
mincemeat a mix of dried fruits, glacé fruits, nuts, spice, sugar and alcohol; most commonly used to make mincemeat tarts.
orange blossom water distilled from orange blossoms.
peanut butter, smooth a creamy blend of ground peanuts, vegetable oil and salt.
peppermint oil from the peppermint plant; often used as a flavouring.

index

conversion chart

measures

One Australian metric measuring cup holds approximately 250ml; one Australian metric tablespoon holds 20ml; one Australian metric teaspoon holds 5ml.

The difference between one country's measuring cups and another's is within a two- or three-teaspoon variance, and will not affect your cooking results. North America, New Zealand and the United Kingdom use a 15ml tablespoon.

All cup and spoon measurements are level. The most accurate way of measuring dry ingredients is to weigh them. When measuring liquids, use a clear glass or plastic jug with the metric markings.

We use large eggs with an average weight of 60g.

dry measures

METRIC	IMPERIAL
15g	½oz
30g	1oz
60g	2oz
90g	3oz
125g	4oz (¼lb)
155g	5oz
185g	6oz
220g	7oz
250g	8oz (½lb)
280g	9oz
315g	10oz
345g	11oz
375g	12oz (¾lb)
410g	13oz
440g	14oz
470g	15oz
500g	16oz (1lb)
750g	24oz (1½lb)
1kg	32oz (2lb)

liquid measures

METRIC	IMPERIAL
30ml	1 fluid oz
60ml	2 fluid oz
100ml	3 fluid oz
125ml	4 fluid oz
150ml	5 fluid oz (¼ pint/1 gill)
190ml	6 fluid oz
250ml	8 fluid oz
300ml	10 fluid oz (½ pint)
500ml	16 fluid oz
600ml	20 fluid oz (1 pint)
1000ml (1 litre)	1¾ pints

length measures

METRIC	IMPERIAL
3mm	⅛in
6mm	¼in
1cm	½in
2cm	¾in
2.5cm	1in
5cm	2in
6cm	2½in
8cm	3in
10cm	4in
13cm	5in
15cm	6in
18cm	7in
20cm	8in
23cm	9in
25cm	10in
28cm	11in
30cm	12in (1ft)

oven temperatures

These oven temperatures are only a guide for conventional ovens. For fan-assisted ovens, check the manufacturer's manual.

	°C (CELSIUS)	°F (FAHRENHEIT)	GAS MARK
Very low	120	250	½
Low	150	275-300	1-2
Moderately low	160	325	3
Moderate	180	350-375	4-5
Moderately hot	200	400	6
Hot	220	425-450	7-8
Very hot	240	475	9